simple acts of kindness

159 Easy Ways to Bring a Smile, Give Comfort, Share Joy, and Inspire a Kinder World

PEGGY HEALY STEARNS, PH.D.

THE
GLENWOOD

TREEHOUSE

This book was inspired by kindness.

The kindness of family, friends, neighbors and strangers.

Kindness during the best of times. And kindness during the darkest days when family and friends kept us afloat and alive.

Simple Acts of Kindness is a tribute to them – and to you, the reader.

Together we can inspire a gentler world

where kindness is valued, appreciated, and encouraged.

CONTENTS

INTRODUCTION

The power of kindness... a warm smile, a thoughtful gesture, a word of encouragement. Each of these small acts has the potential to brighten someone's day, to offer hope, to remind them that they are valued.

Kindness is more than something we do on occasion. It is a way of life. By actively seeking opportunities to be kind, we cultivate a mindset of compassion and generosity that enriches both our lives and the lives of those around us.

In a world that can feel hurried and divided, simple acts of kindness remind us of our shared humanity and our ability to make a difference.

ABOUT THIS BOOK

This book offers simple, accessible ways to spread joy, offer comfort, and uplift those around you.

The early chapters provide insight into the power of kindness, address common barriers, and suggest ideas for incorporating kindness in ways that feel authentic and natural. Whether you're an extrovert who loves engaging with people or someone who prefers quieter, behind-the-scenes gestures, you'll find ideas that align with your strengths and lifestyle.

The heart of the book is the list of 159 simple acts of kindness grouped into categories that help you find ideas that work well in different settings—at home, among friends, in the work-place, in the broader neighborhood and community, and with strangers. It also addresses special topics like kindness and compassion in challenging times and the importance of self-care.

As you read through these pages, I hope you feel inspired to embrace kindness in ways that are meaningful to you. Start small. Start today. A kind word, a helping hand, a moment of patience—these are the building blocks of a kinder world.

1

WHY KINDNESS MATTERS

K indness has the power to soften even the hardest days. A small, unexpected act of care can remind us that we are seen, valued, and not alone. It can change a moment, a day, or even a life.

When we choose kindness, we are not only helping others; we are also creating a life filled with deeper connections, gratitude, and a sense of purpose.

THE SCIENCE OF KINDNESS

Kindness isn't just a feel-good concept—it has measurable benefits backed by science. Research shows that practicing kindness enhances both mental and physical well-being, strengthens relationships, and even contributes to longevity.

When we engage in acts of kindness, our brain releases a cocktail of feel-good chemicals, including oxytocin, serotonin, and dopamine. These neurotransmitters contribute to reduced stress, increased happiness, and a greater sense of connection to others. Studies using MRI scans have shown that the brain's reward system lights up when we perform or even witness acts of kindness, much the same way the brain responds to pleasurable experiences like eating or social bonding (Zak, 2017; Klimecki et al., 2013).

Kindness has other significant health benefits. Research from the Mayo Clinic and other institutions suggests that acts of kindness can:

- **Lower blood pressure** – Oxytocin, often called the "love hormone," helps reduce stress and lower blood pressure (Dfarhud et al., 2014).
- **Strengthen the immune system** – Positive emotions linked to kindness contribute to better overall health (Post, 2005).
- **Reduce pain** – Engaging in kind acts has been shown to increase endorphins, the body's natural painkillers (Raposa et al., 2016).
- **Increase lifespan** – Studies suggest that people who regularly help others have a higher life expectancy than those who don't (Post, 2005).

Additional studies reinforce findings that acts of kindness significantly improve mental health by reducing anxiety, depression, and stress. Research published in the *Journal of Social Psychology* found that people who performed at least one act of kindness a day for seven days reported increased happiness (Layous et al., 2012). Another study from the University of British Columbia revealed that acts of kindness can reduce social anxiety, making it easier for people to connect and form relationships (Alden et al., 2017).

Science confirms what we've long known intuitively—kindness benefits both the giver and the receiver. By incorporating small acts of kindness into daily life, we enhance our well-being, improve our relationships, and contribute to a healthier, happier world.

SMALL ACTIONS, BIG IMPACT

It's easy to underestimate the power of a simple act of kindness. After all, how much difference can a small gesture really make? The answer is: more than we know. A kind word at the right moment can restore someone's faith in humanity. A handwritten note can become a cherished keepsake. A listening ear can help ease a heavy burden.

We don't need grand gestures or deep pockets to make an impact. A little thoughtfulness goes a long way. Even the smallest actions—holding the door for someone, offering a sincere compliment, checking in on a friend—can shift the energy of a moment, a day, or even a life.

THE RIPPLE EFFECT

Kindness has a way of expanding far beyond its original source. When we practice kindness, we plant seeds in places we may never see.

Research from the University of California, Berkeley, found that when people observe kind behavior, they are more likely to engage in kind acts themselves.

Perhaps you let someone go ahead of you in line at the grocery store. That person, feeling uplifted, decides to pay it forward by leaving an extra-large tip for their server at lunch. The server, moved by this unexpected kindness, goes home in a better mood and takes extra time to help their child with homework. That child, feeling supported, enters school the next day with more confidence and extends kindness to a struggling classmate.

This "pay-it-forward" effect can create a ripple of goodwill that extends far beyond the initial act, influencing communities, workplaces, and even global movements.

In a world that often feels divided and uncertain, those ripples matter more than ever. What starts as a simple gesture can grow into something much larger—a movement of kindness that transforms relationships, workplaces, and communities.

2

WHEN KINDNESS IS HARD

Sometimes kindness is hard. We may be busy, on a tight budget, or feel overwhelmed with challenges in our own lives. Other times we may worry that our kindness will be misinterpreted, or that our actions won't make a difference.

This book suggests practical ways to navigate those challenges by offering small but meaningful acts of kindness that fit into any lifestyle.

BUSY SCHEDULES: FINDING TIME FOR KINDNESS

One of the biggest challenges people cite is lack of time. With packed calendars and endless to-do lists, kindness can feel like one more thing to fit in. But here's the good news: kindness doesn't have to be time-consuming. It isn't about grand gestures; it's about small, meaningful moments woven into everyday life.

Many acts of kindness take only seconds—a kind word to a coworker, a quick text to check on a friend, holding the door for someone.

One way to fit kindness into a busy schedule is to attach it to something you already do. If you're commuting, let someone merge in front of you with a wave. If you're heading out for a walk, take a moment to smile at a passerby. If you grab a morning coffee, consider picking up an extra for a coworker.

Kindness doesn't have to require extra hours in the day. If you shift your perspective to see kindness as part of how you move through the world, it becomes easier to find time.

FINANCIAL CONCERNS

You may be innately generous and want to give but have a limited budget. Fortunately, many of the most meaningful acts of kindness cost nothing.

Generosity can take many forms—giving your time, your attention, your encouragement, or your skills. A heartfelt compliment, a sincere "thank you," or simply listening with full presence can have just as much impact as any material gift.

If you do want to give in tangible ways but are on a budget, there are still plenty of options. Baking extra cookies to share, donating items you no longer need, or writing a thoughtful note are all acts of kindness that cost little to nothing. The value of kindness isn't measured in dollars—it's measured in care.

FEAR OF OVERSTEPPING BOUNDARIES

Another barrier to kindness is the fear of how it will be received. We may hesitate because we don't want to intrude. We worry that checking in on someone may seem nosy, or that offering help may come across as implying they can't handle something on their own.

What if your offer of help is declined? What if your kind words feel awkward? What if the other person doesn't respond as you hoped? This can make acts of kindness feel unnatural, as though we are crossing an invisible boundary.

While it's important to respect boundaries, there are ways to be kind that honor both care and autonomy. Instead of assuming, simply ask. "Would it be helpful if I..." or "I'd love to do this for you, but no pressure at all" leaves space for the other person to accept or decline comfortably.

Sometimes, silent gestures—like leaving a note of encouragement or doing something kind anonymously—are a way to offer support without making the recipient feel put on the spot. Thoughtful acts of kindness consider not just what we want to give, but how the other person may best receive it.

FEELING UNAPPRECIATED

At times, we may feel discouraged when acts of kindness go unnoticed or unacknowledged. We hold the door, but no one says thank you. We go out of our way to help, and no one seems to care. It's understandable to want kindness to be recognized, but the true power of kindness lies in giving without expectation.

When we choose to be kind, we do it because it aligns with who we are, not for external validation. Appreciation is wonderful, but it shouldn't be the driving force behind kindness.

If someone seems indifferent, it doesn't mean your kindness wasn't felt. It may have reached them at a moment when they needed it most but weren't able to express it. Often, kindness has a delayed impact—someone may not acknowledge it in the moment but later reflect on how much it meant to them.

ASSUMING SOMEONE ELSE WILL HANDLE IT

It's easy to think, "Someone else will step in." Someone else will compliment the shy coworker. Someone else will hold the door. Someone else will check in on the elderly neighbor.

Sometimes someone else will. Other times, you can be that someone. Just be aware of opportunities. Instead of waiting for kindness to happen, you can be the one to create it.

TAKING CARE OF YOURSELF

If we want to spread kindness, we need to be kind to ourselves as well. Kindness should never come at the expense of our well-being.

Setting healthy boundaries is essential – saying no when needed doesn't make you unkind; it allows you to give from a place of abundance rather than depletion. Giving yourself permission to rest is just as important as giving to others.

When we are tired or stressed or overwhelmed, our acts of kindness may come across as grudging instead of generous, and the recipient may feel uncomfortable and worry they have overstepped or inconvenienced us.

Recognizing that self-care is an act of kindness allows us to recharge and show up more fully for others. Taking care of mind and body isn't selfish; it's a necessary foundation for spreading kindness in a sustainable way.

3
KINDNESS YOUR WAY

People express kindness in different ways. The most meaningful and sustainable acts of kindness are the ones that feel natural to you. When kindness aligns with your personality, strengths, and lifestyle, it doesn't feel like an obligation—it becomes an effortless, joyful part of who you are.

TAP INTO YOUR TALENTS

Everyone has unique strengths, and kindness can be an extension of what you already do well. What comes easily to you can brighten someone's day.

If you love to cook, consider making an extra meal or batch of cookies to share with a friend or neighbor. If writing is your strength, you could send an uplifting note, while those with artistic talent might share a heartfelt drawing. If you have a green thumb, you could plant flowers in a community space or share fresh produce from your gardens. A musician might volunteer to play for family and friends or a community group. A teacher can offer to mentor someone.

When you use your natural talents to spread kindness, it becomes an extension of who you are and what you love. What seems small or effortless to you can be a tremendous gift to someone else.

HONOR YOUR SOCIAL PREFERENCES

People thrive and are best able to give in different social settings. If you are energized by face-to-face connection, you may find joy in engaging directly with others. Stopping in to see a friend or family member is warm and personal. A friendly conversation with someone who seems lonely can brighten the day. Volunteering at a community center, soup kitchen, or animal shelter can be a great way to give back.

If you feel more comfortable being kind from a distance, there are plenty of ways to contribute without direct social interaction. Writing positive online reviews for small businesses or authors you appreciate spreads encouragement. A thoughtful text or email to check in on someone might be just as meaningful as a visit. Donating to a cause you care about can make a big impact. Leaving a generous tip when dining out or ordering delivery is an easy way to spread kindness.

Some people enjoy offering kindness without recognition. If this resonates with you, consider sending an anonymous thank-you note to someone who has made a difference in your life, paying for someone's coffee or meal in a drive-thru, or donating essential supplies to a shelter or food bank without attaching your name.

BE AUTHENTIC

Kindness is most powerful when it comes from a place of sincerity. There's no "right" way to be kind—what matters is choosing acts that feel comfortable and natural. Just show up as yourself and give in a way that aligns with your values and personality.

4

MAKE KINDNESS A LIFESTYLE

Kindness is not just something we do—it's a way of being. When kindness becomes a natural part of our daily lives, it transforms the way we experience the world and how others experience us.

START SMALL AND CREATE A POSITIVE FEEDBACK LOOP

One of the easiest ways to make kindness a habit is to start small. Just as tiny shifts in routine can lead to lasting habits, small acts of kindness can create a momentum that builds over time.

Holding the door open, offering a genuine compliment, or checking in on a friend takes mere seconds but can have a profound impact. The beauty of these small gestures is that they create a positive feedback loop—when we are kind, we feel good, and that encourages us to continue.

A simple way to reinforce this habit is by setting small kindness goals. Try committing to one intentional act of kindness per day. Over time, this practice becomes second nature—an integral part of who we are.

GRATITUDE IS AN ACT OF KINDNESS

Gratitude itself is an act of kindness. Expressing thanks—whether through words, a note, or a heartfelt gesture—reminds people that their kindness makes a difference and encourages them to continue.

When we make gratitude a habit, we begin to see kindness everywhere—a friend who listens, a coworker who offers support, a stranger who lets us merge in traffic. Recognizing these small acts of kindness not only encourages the giver but can also inspire us to pass it forward.

A WAY OF LIFE

When kindness becomes part of our daily rhythm, we begin to see the world through a lens of compassion, noticing opportunities to uplift others in the smallest ways. And in doing so, we create a life that is richer, fuller, and more connected.

The beauty of kindness is that it's self-sustaining. The more we practice it, the more natural it becomes. The more we give, the more we receive. And the more we recognize kindness around us, the more it grows. Little by little, kindness transforms from *something we do* to *something we are.*

5
159 SIMPLE ACTS OF KINDNESS

The following lists are designed to spark inspiration and help you recognize everyday opportunities to spread kindness in ways that feel authentic.

If you are reading this book, chances are you already practice many of these gestures—and likely have additional ideas. My hope is that these suggestions introduce new possibilities that resonate with you and encourage even more moments of kindness in your daily life.

To help you find ideas that work well in different settings, suggestions are organized into seven categories:

- At Home
- Extended Family & Friends
- Neighborhood & Community
- Workplace: Creating a Culture of Kindness
- Kindness to Strangers
- Kindness & Compassion in Tough Times
- Self-Kindness: Taking Care of Yourself

Categories are flexible and overlap. Many gestures in one category will likely be equally welcome and comforting in other settings, so be sure to explore all the lists.

AT HOME

1. **Start the day with a kind word** – A cheerful "good morning" can set a positive tone.
2. **Serve coffee, tea or juice in bed** – Surprise your loved one with a favorite morning beverage.
3. **Get up early** – To see a family member off on a trip or a challenging day.
4. **Offer a hug or pat on the back** – Physical reassurance can be comforting.
5. **Give a genuine compliment** – Let family members know they are appreciated.
6. **Leave a nice note** – Place an uplifting message on the mirror or fridge or packed in a lunch.
7. **Offer help** – Assist with a chore around the house.
8. **Provide emotional support** – For a child or partner navigating a school or professional challenge.
9. **Wash the car** – Surprise someone who is heading off for a special event.
10. **Be responsive** – Answer calls and text messages as soon as practical.
11. **Ask, "How was your day?"** – Check in with everyone.
12. **Listen carefully** – Your attention tells family they are important.
13. **Cheer them on** – Encourage family members who are pursuing their goals and dreams.
14. **Be patient** – With family members struggling to learn something new.

15. **Give praise** – For jobs well done, school or athletic performance, or professional accomplishments.
16. **Display their work** – Post on the refrigerator, hang on a wall, set on a table or shelf.
17. **Bring home flowers** – From a market or shop, your garden, or wildflowers picked along the road.
18. **Prepare a favorite meal** – A delicious way to create connection and shared memories.
19. **Set the table nicely** – Let family know that meals together are important.
20. **Put away phones during family time** – Be fully present during conversations.
21. **Stay at the dinner table longer** – Give everyone time to talk about their day or anything of special interest.
22. **Celebrate small achievements** – Getting to the gym, learning something new, or navigating a tough day.
23. **Say "thank you" more often** – Express gratitude for the little things we often take for granted.
24. **Do something together without a screen** – Piece together a puzzle, play a board game, or go for a walk.
25. **Be an advocate** – When a family member is facing a health challenge, do your best to stay informed, follow their healing path, and support them.
26. **Stay up late** – To greet someone coming home from a trip or a challenging day.
27. **Light their way** – Make sure the porch light or entryway is lit when they arrive home after dark.
28. **Keep your promises** – Let family know they can depend on you.

1. **Check in** – Send a quick text to let someone know you're thinking of them.
2. **Make a phone call** – For someone who prefers a more personal connection, even if you only leave a voicemail.
3. **Invite a friend to relax on your porch** – Just to chat and share a cup of tea or glass of water.
4. **Ask a friend on a walk** – A casual, low-pressure way to spend time together.
5. **Invite others into the conversation** – Encourage quieter individuals to share their thoughts.
6. **Offer to do an errand** – Pick up groceries or drop off dry cleaning.
7. **Provide transportation** – Help a friend or family member get to an appointment or event.
8. **Remember special dates** – Birthdays, anniversaries, or important life events.
9. **Send a handwritten letter or card** – A personal touch in a digital world.
10. **Express your message through art** – A hand-drawn illustration can be a memorable and cherished keepsake.
11. **Share a photo** – A meaningful memory sent via text, email or print.
12. **Leave a surprise on their doorstep** – A plant, a treat, a product sample they might enjoy.
13. **Offer to babysit** – Give Mom or Dad or the child's caretaker a short break or a night out.
14. **Walk the dog** – When the pet's human is not up to the task.

15. **Offer to check a friend's house when they're away** – Knowing their home is safe will ease their mind.
16. **Leave a snack** – For a friend arriving home late from a long trip.
17. **Invite a friend to join your club** – Book club, garden club, quilting club – any group you might enjoy together.
18. **Organize a cookie exchange** – In advance of the holidays, meet to share your favorite home-baked cookies.
19. **Lend a book you love** – Include a note on why you thought they'd enjoy it.
20. **Help with consumer research** – For someone planning a purchase or trip.
21. **Make a personalized playlist** – Songs from good times you've shared or music you think they will enjoy.
22. **Share your musical talent** – If you're a musician, do a live mini-concert or record yourself playing a special song, even if it's just your practice session.
23. **Celebrate their successes** – Promotions, graduations, and small wins all deserve recognition.
24. **Share the bounty of your vegetable garden** – A fresh homegrown tomato, lettuce, zucchini, herbs, or whatever is in season.
25. **Pick some flowers from your garden** – Even a few stems are a thoughtful gift.
26. **Share seeds or seedlings** – Help family and friends start their own gardens.
27. **Play a game** – Offer to play a card or board game they enjoy – even if it's not your favorite.
28. **Suggest you try something new together** – A painting class, a yoga session, or a community event.

29. **Keep them posted** – Share news of upcoming events that might interest them.
30. **Save a seat** – If you arrive early at an open event, save a seat for your friend.
31. **Bring an extra chair** – Offer to bring an extra lawn chair to an outdoor performance.
32. **Be there** – Make the extra effort to show up at a party or gathering.
33. **Be a good listener** – Sometimes people just need to talk.

NEIGHBORHOOD & COMMUNITY

1. **Greet your neighbors** – Even a smile or a wave supports a sense of community.
2. **Bring in your neighbor's trash can** – Especially helpful if they are under the weather or unusually busy.
3. **Check on elderly or isolated neighbors** – Offer to run errands, bring groceries, or simply chat.
4. **Help with yard work** – Rake leaves, mow, shovel snow, or water plants for someone who might need assistance.
5. **Collect mail and packages when they're away** – Help keep your neighbor's deliveries safe.
6. **Offer to walk the dog** – Especially helpful for those with limited mobility or busy schedules.
7. **Suggest a carpool** – A great way to help neighbors with busy schedules while reducing gas use and environmental impacts.
8. **Help plan a neighborhood or community event** – Entertainment, food, or informational meeting to bring people together.

9. **Organize a neighborhood cleanup** – Gather a group to pick up litter and beautify shared spaces.
10. **Start a community garden** – Flowers, native plants, or a vegetable garden in shared areas.
11. **Add artistic flair to a public space** – Bring beauty to a common area with colorful murals, uplifting designs, or creative enhancements.
12. **Support community festivals and cultural events** – Even small local events help build a sense of community.
13. **Drop books or magazines at a local laundry mat** – A nice diversion for patrons waiting for laundry.
14. **Donate unused household items** – Give to a local shelter, community center, or neighbor in need.
15. **Start a Little Free Library** – Encourage everyone to give and take books.
16. **Volunteer to read at the library or online** – Storytime for children or other community reading programs.
17. **Offer to translate** – If you're multilingual, a great way to help someone who struggles with a language barrier.
18. **Thank your mail carriers and delivery drivers** – Leave out a snack or bottle of water to let them know their service is appreciated.
19. **Drop off a treat at the fire hall or police station** – Include a handwritten thank you.
20. **Address people by name** – It shows respect and appreciation beyond their role or service.
21. **Sponsor a kindness rock garden** – Paint uplifting messages on rocks and place them in public spaces around your neighborhood.

22. **Support local businesses** – Shop locally, leave positive reviews, and recommend them to friends.
23. **Welcome a new family** – Introduce yourself, share community resources, or invite them over.

WORKPLACE: CREATING A CULTURE OF KINDNESS

1. **Say "good morning" to everyone** – A cheerful way to start the day.
2. **Bring in a treat to share** – Some fruit, a batch of cookies, or coffee for the team.
3. **Offer help** – Answer questions for a coworker who expresses frustration with a new task.
4. **Offer to proofread a colleague's work** – A second set of eyes can boost clarity and confidence.
5. **Cover for someone** – If a colleague needs an unexpected break.
6. **Leave an encouraging sticky note on a desk** – A positive message can change someone's day.
7. **Listen without interrupting** – Giving someone your full attention shows respect and support.
8. **Be mindful of noise levels** – Respect quiet spaces and use headphones when needed.
9. **Compliment a colleague's work** – Acknowledge a job well done in person or via text or email.
10. **Praise someone in a meeting** – Publicly acknowledge a coworker's good work.
11. **Respect everyone's time in meetings** – Arrive on time and keep discussions productive.
12. **Celebrate birthdays and milestones** – Even a simple note can make someone feel valued.

13. **Follow up with a colleague who's been out** – If someone has been sick or dealing with a challenge at home, let them know you care.
14. **Keep the break room clean** – A little effort shows respect and makes the space more pleasant for everyone.
15. **Write a thank-you note** – Let a coworker know you appreciate their efforts.
16. **Share an inspiring article or quote** – Something that will speak to and uplift coworkers.
17. **Be inclusive** – Invite someone who often eats alone to join your lunch group.
18. **Welcome a new colleague** – Offer a tour, introduce them to co-workers, check in to see if they need anything.
19. **Express gratitude to support staff** – Thank janitors, receptionists, IT, and administrative teams.
20. **Respect work-life boundaries** – Avoid sending late-night emails or texts unless urgent.

KINDNESS TO STRANGERS

1. **Smile at strangers** – A simple smile can make a difference in someone's day.
2. **Hold the door** – A small gesture that is almost always appreciated.
3. **Offer your seat** – On a bus, train, or in a waiting area, give up your seat to someone who may need it more.
4. **Say "thank you" to a service worker** – Express appreciation to cashiers, janitors, or security staff.
5. **Compliment a stranger** – A kind word about their outfit, smile, or work can be uplifting.

6. **Share your umbrella** – Offer to shield someone from the rain.
7. **Pick up litter** – Help keep your community clean.
8. **Capture a special moment** – Ask someone struggling with a selfie if they'd like you to take a photo.
9. **Leave coins at a vending machine** – A small surprise for the next patron.
10. **Hold the elevator doors open** – Give someone a few extra seconds to make it.
11. **Help a shopper**– If you're familiar with a store or market, help a fellow shopper find an item.
12. **Reach up** – Offer to grab an item on a high shelf for someone who can't reach.
13. **Make room** – Notice when others are trying to get down a crowded aisle and shift your cart to let them pass.
14. **Let someone go ahead in the checkout line** – Especially if they seem rushed or have fewer items.
15. **Help carry the load** – When you see someone struggling with packages or baggage, offer to help.
16. **Return a shopping cart** – Even if it's not yours, it helps keep the lot safe and lightens the load for employees.
17. **Help someone find their car** – Yes, it happens. In large lots, people sometimes forget where they parked – especially if cars are covered in snow.
18. **Hold back from honking in traffic** – A little patience can ease someone's stress.
19. **Give up a parking spot** – If someone else is eyeing the same place, hold back and wave them in.
20. **Help someone cross the street** – If appropriate, offer an arm, or simply walk nearby to buffer traffic.

21. **Respect pedestrian crosswalks** – Give people time to reach the other side before rushing by.
22. **Share the road** – Give bicyclists a comfortable berth to help keep them safe.

KINDNESS & COMPASSION IN TOUGH TIMES

When people face challenges due to illness, grief, financial hardship, or personal struggles, small acts of kindness can be a lifeline. While many of the gestures above can offer meaningful support, the suggestions below focus specifically on providing comfort during life's toughest moments.

1. **Reach out** – Let those in crisis know you are thinking of them and available to listen and help.
2. **Offer to do errands** – Grocery shopping, pharmacy pickups, or childcare.
3. **Accompany them to appointments** – Offer to drive or sit with them for medical visits or other important meetings.
4. **Take a shift at the hospital** – Give the caretaker time to rest and recharge.
5. **Drop off a meal** – A practical way to support someone in need.
6. **Send a care package** – Thoughtful items like snacks, books, or cozy socks.
7. **Provide a distraction** – Invite them for a walk, movie night, or other low-pressure activity.
8. **Welcome people into your home** – A cozy space and good company can be a refreshing change.
9. **Drop by their home if they prefer** – Let them choose the setting that is most comfortable for them.

10. **Lend a hand with household chores** – Laundry, cleaning, or yard work.
11. **Help someone find a job** – Share job leads, review resumés, roleplay interviews, or simply offer encouragement.
12. **Sit with someone who is grieving** – Sometimes just being there is a great comfort.
13. **Share stories** – Enjoy the retelling of favorite memories.
14. **Send a handwritten card** – A tangible reminder that they are not alone.
15. **Help with holiday or birthday preparations** – Assist in making special days feel lighter and more joyful.
16. **Offer financial assistance if practical** – Offer to cover a specific expense or make an open-ended donation.
17. **Be patient and consistent** – Hard times don't pass overnight. Keep checking in, even after things seem to settle.
18. **Let them know they are not alone** -- Answer calls and texts and be available in person when practical.
19. **Listen without giving advice** – Sometimes people just need to talk.

SELF-KINDNESS: TAKING CARE OF YOURSELF

1. **Speak kindly to yourself** – Avoid negative self-talk.
2. **Give yourself permission to rest** – You don't have to be productive all the time.
3. **Nourish your body** – Choose foods that fuel and sustain you.
4. **Treat yourself** – Even something small like a favorite book, snack, or activity.

5. **Take a break from social media** – Unplug and allow your mind some quiet.
6. **Prioritize your mental health** – Make time to relax and seek support when needed.
7. **Nurture your inner child** – Do something fun, relaxing, and purely for enjoyment.
8. **Dance** – Put on some favorite music and get in the groove.
9. **Exercise** – Any activity that makes you feel happy and alive.
10. **Relax in nature** – Even if all you do is gaze at the sky, trees, birds, water, whatever natural beauty surrounds you.
11. **Laugh** – Watch a funny movie or video, read a humorous book, hang out with a lighthearted friend.
12. **Celebrate your own achievements** – Even little victories deserve recognition.
13. **Smile at yourself in the mirror** – Appreciate all the things that make you special.
14. **Unwind with gratitude** – As your day ends, let moments that lifted your spirits comfort you as you drift off to sleep.

FINAL THOUGHTS

Thank you for joining me in seeking ways to bring more kindness into our world. Your efforts—no matter how big or small—contribute to a culture where kindness is valued, appreciated, and encouraged.

Kindness does not require grand gestures or endless resources. It is found in the smallest moments: a smile, a helping hand, a word of encouragement. These little acts of kindness add up, creating ripples that extend far beyond what we see. By choosing to be kind in everyday moments, we can inspire others to do the same, fostering a cycle of goodwill that can help transform individuals and communities.

If this book has left you with one takeaway, I hope it is this: kindness is within your power every day. Even simple acts of kindness can make a meaningful difference.

Start small. Start today. Together, through our collective efforts, we can inspire a gentler and more compassionate world.

REFERENCES

Aknin, L. B., Dunn, E. W., & Norton, M. I. (2012). Happiness runs in a circular motion: Evidence for a positive feedback loop between prosocial spending and happiness. *Journal of Happiness Studies, 13*(2), 347-355.

Alden, L. E., Trew, J. L., & Plasencia, M. L. (2017). Helping others helps anxiety? Examining the effect of prosocial behavior on social anxiety. *Motivation and Emotion, 41*(1), 44-56.

Brown, B. (2012). *Daring greatly: How the courage to be vulnerable transforms the way we live, love, parent, and lead.* Avery.

Dfarhud, D., Malmir, M., & Khanahmadi, M. (2014). Happiness & health: The biological factors—systematic review article. *Iranian Journal of Public Health, 43*(11), 1468-1477.

Dunn, E. W., Aknin, L. B., & Norton, M. I. (2008). Spending money on others promotes happiness. *Science, 319*(5870), 1687-1688.

Fowler, J. H., & Christakis, N. A. (2010). Cooperative behavior cascades in human social networks. *Proceedings of the National Academy of Sciences, 107*(12), 5334-5338.

Fredrickson, B. L. (2009). *Positivity: Top-notch research reveals the 3-to-1 ratio that will change your life.* Harmony.

Haidt, J. (2006). *The happiness hypothesis: Finding modern truth in ancient wisdom.* Basic Books.

Hossein, A. (2023, November 25). Ripple effect. *Medium.* https://medium.com/@amirhossein101/ripple-effect-a06b55545665

Klimecki, O. M., Leiberg, S., Lamm, C., & Singer, T. (2013). Functional neural plasticity and associated changes in positive affect after compassion training. *Cerebral Cortex, 23*(7), 1552-1561.

Layous, K., Nelson, S. K., Oberle, E., Schonert-Reichl, K. A., & Lyubomirsky, S. (2012). Kindness counts: Prompting prosocial behavior in preadolescents boosts peer acceptance and well-being. *PLoS One, 7*(12), e51380.

Lyubomirsky, S. (2007). *The how of happiness: A new approach to getting the life you want.* Penguin.

Post, S. G. (2005). Altruism, happiness, and health: It's good to be good. *International Journal of Behavioral Medicine, 12*(2), 66-77.

Post, S. G. (2011). *The hidden gifts of helping: How the power of giving, compassion, and hope can get us through hard times.* Jossey-Bass.

Raposa, E. B., Laws, H. B., & Ansell, E. B. (2016). Prosocial behavior mitigates the negative effects of stress in everyday life. *Clinical Psychological Science, 4*(4), 691-698.

Ricard, M. (2015). *Altruism: The power of compassion to change yourself and the world*. Little, Brown and Company.

Seligman, M. E. P. (2011). *Flourish: A visionary new understanding of happiness and well-being*. Atria Books.

Seppala, E. (2016). *The happiness track: How to apply the science of happiness to accelerate your success*. HarperOne.

Thaler, R. H., & Sunstein, C. R. (2008). *Nudge: Improving decisions about health, wealth, and happiness*. Yale University Press.

Vild, G. (2024, October 31). *What you can do to spark a gentler, kinder world*. Psychology Today.

Williamson, M. (1992). *A return to love: Reflections on the principles of A Course in Miracles*. HarperOne.

Zak, P. J. (2017). The neuroscience of trust. *Harvard Business Review, 95*(1), 84-90.

www.ingramcontent.com/pod-product-compliance
Lightning Source LLC
Chambersburg PA
CBHW071823050426
42335CB00063BA/1788

9 7 8 1 9 6 7 8 1 0 0 1 7